Colorblind Images
black & white
photography

Joseph Fleming

Decades of living around accomplished artists producing absolutely phenomenal quality work has taught that we are capable of greatness. It is possible to meet our destiny and become it. Experiencing excellence done with such apparent magical ease and humble selfless gratification is inspiration for this original photography.

Being colorblind gives an advantage when composing black & white… less confusion.

This special collection exhibits the lonely freedom of a hidden perspective selected from thousands of captures during years of travels. All images were framed in the camera and presented without edits, genuine as seen through the lens. Panchromatic conversion by unique proprietary process.

Fine art prints and custom work available.

info@ BEACHNOISE.com

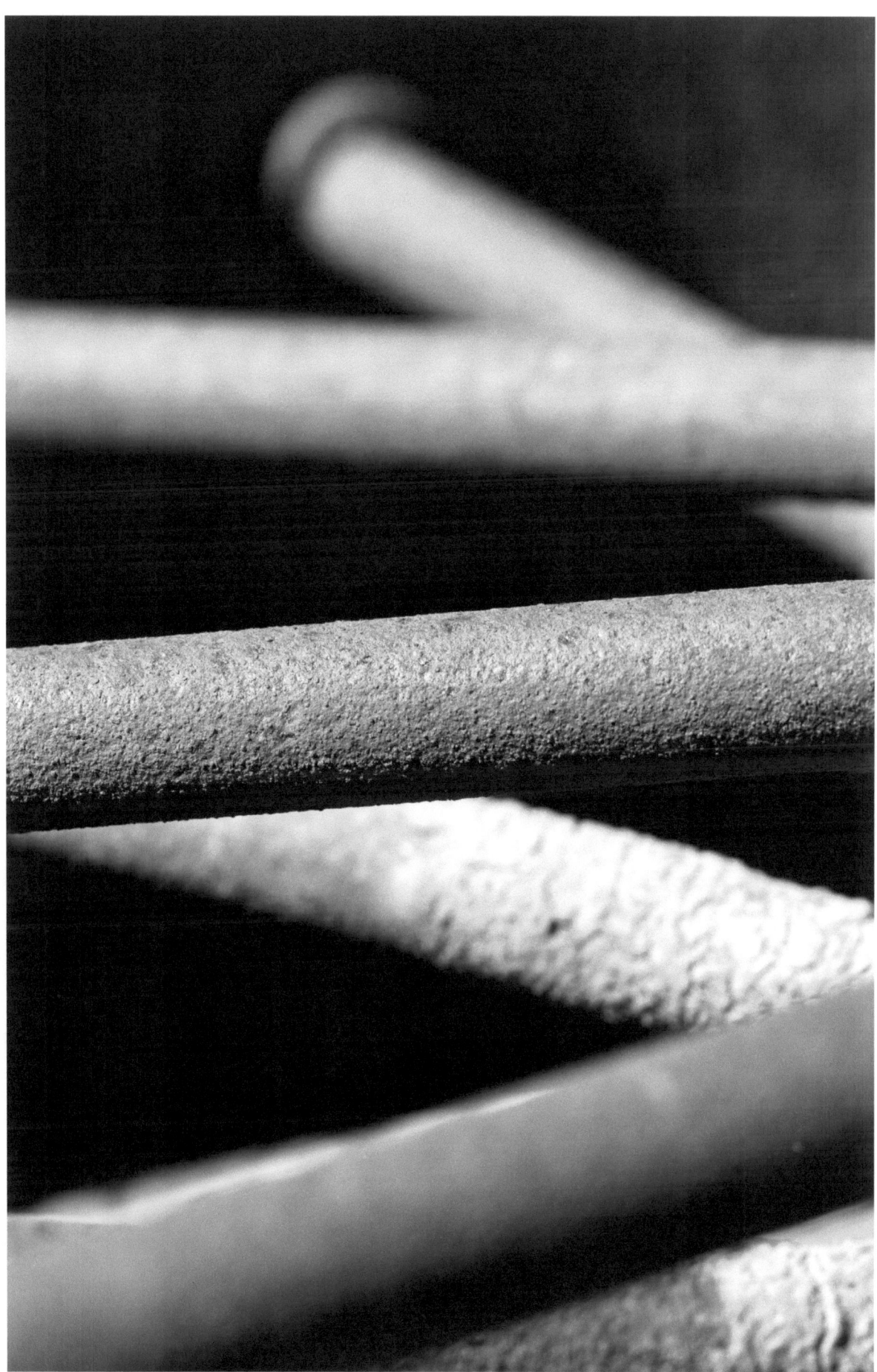

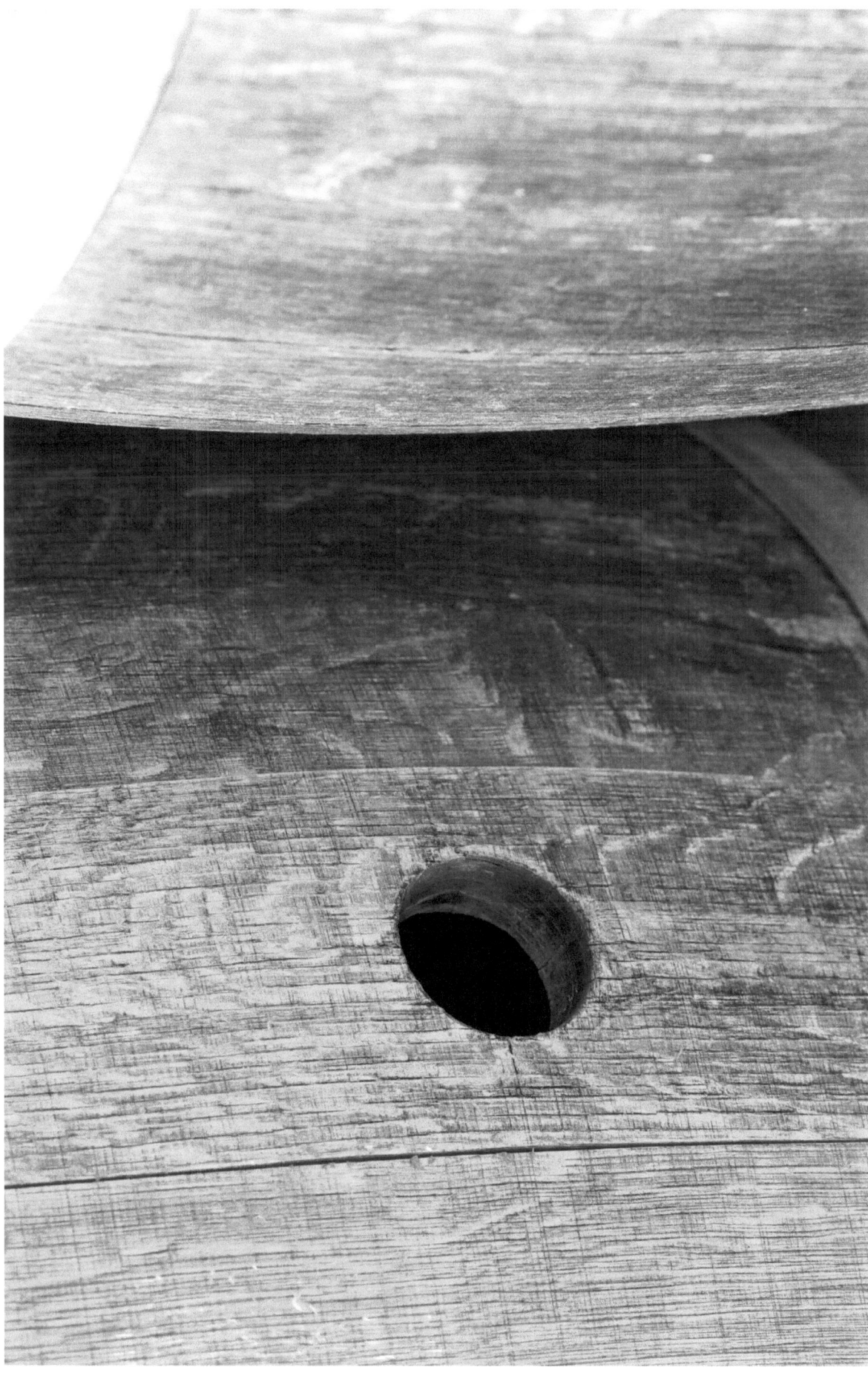

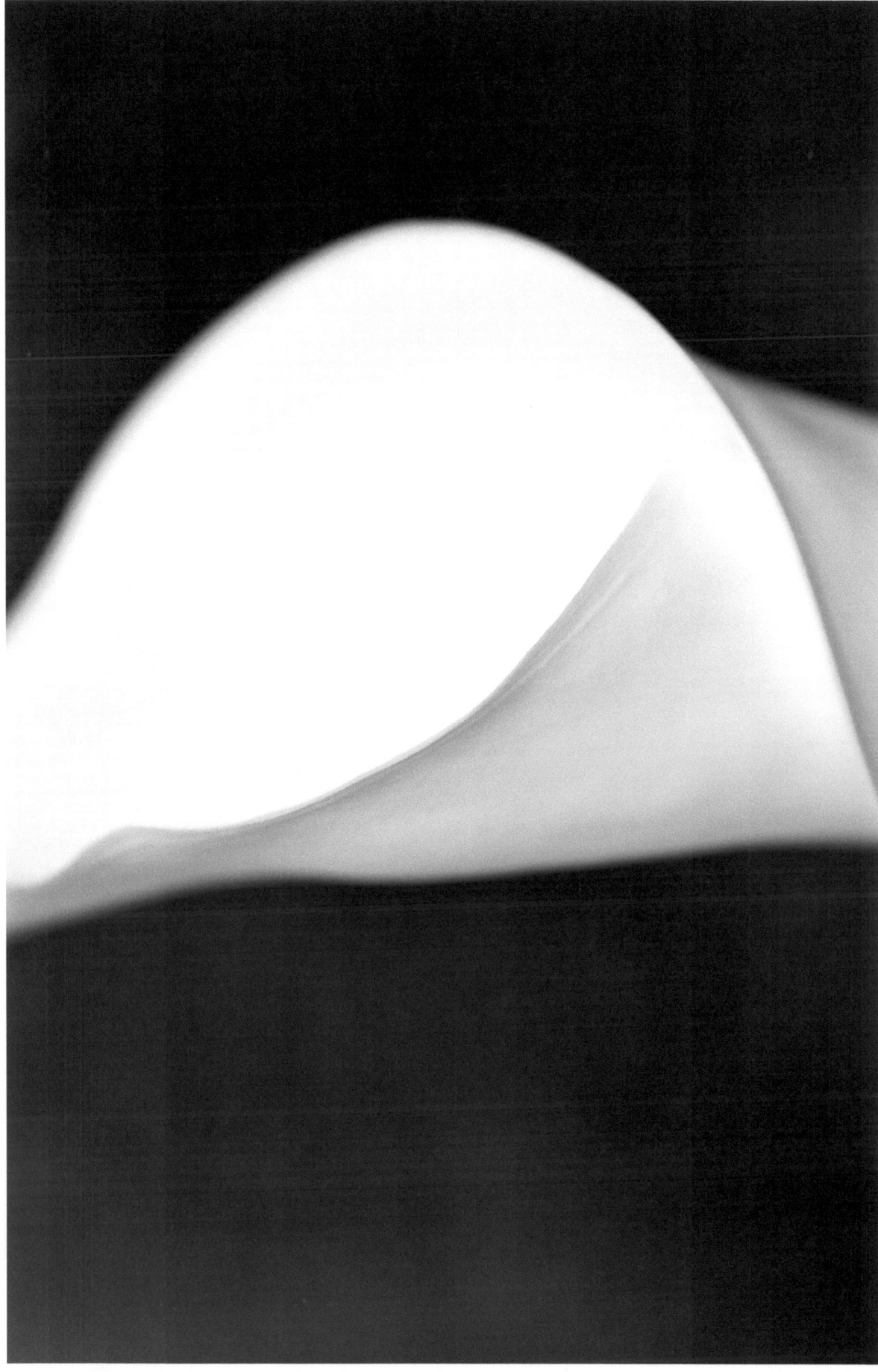

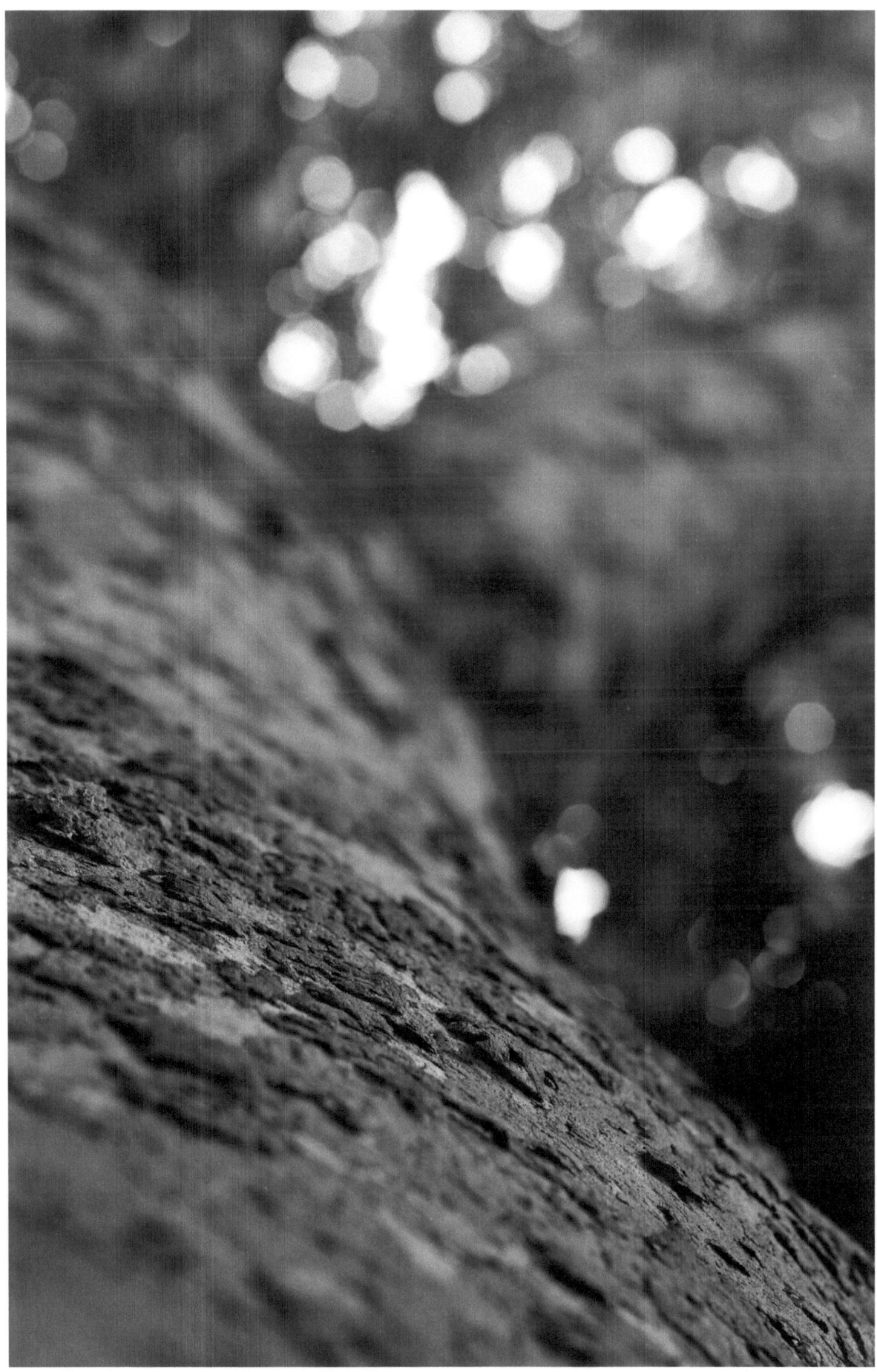

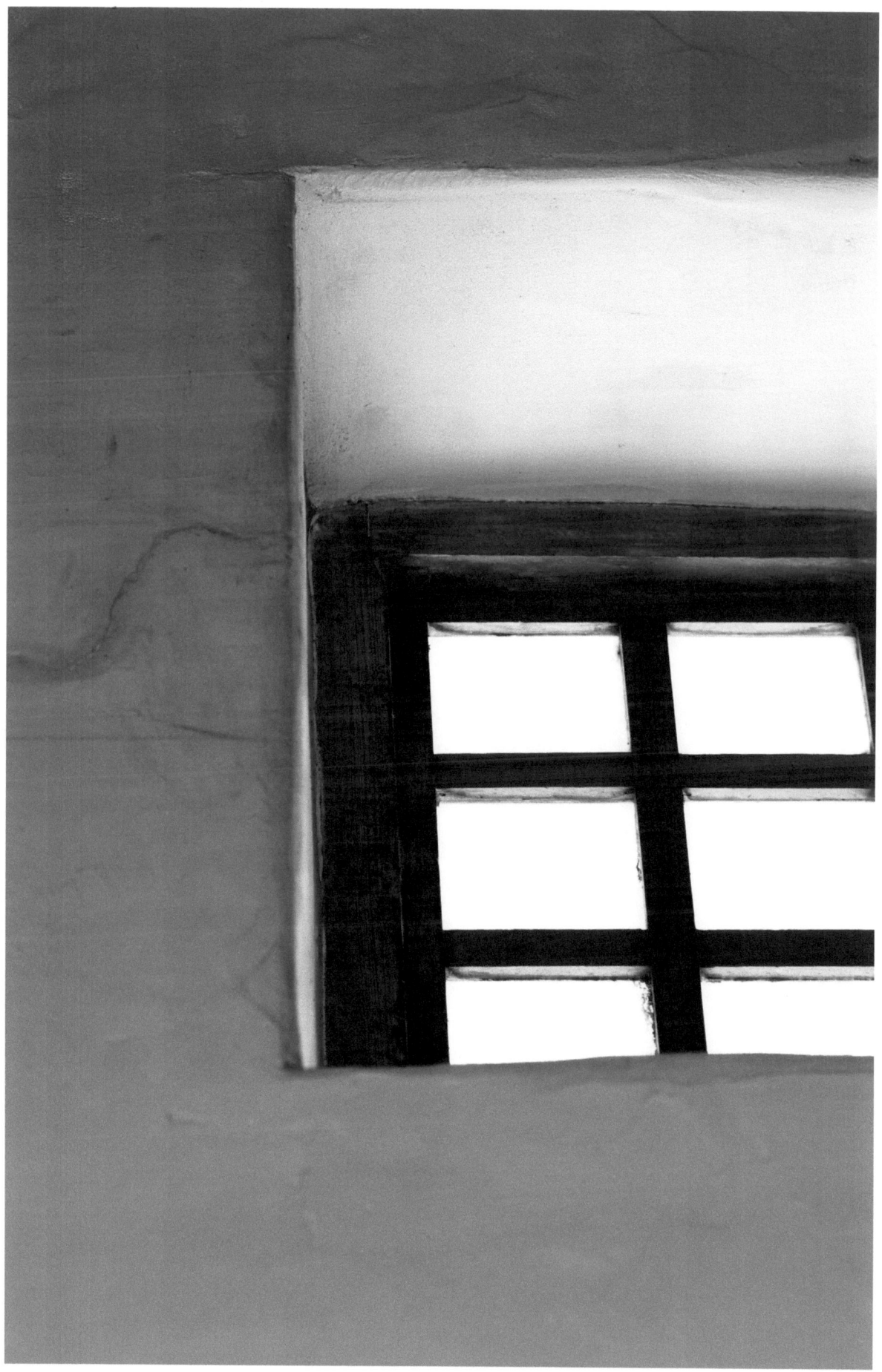

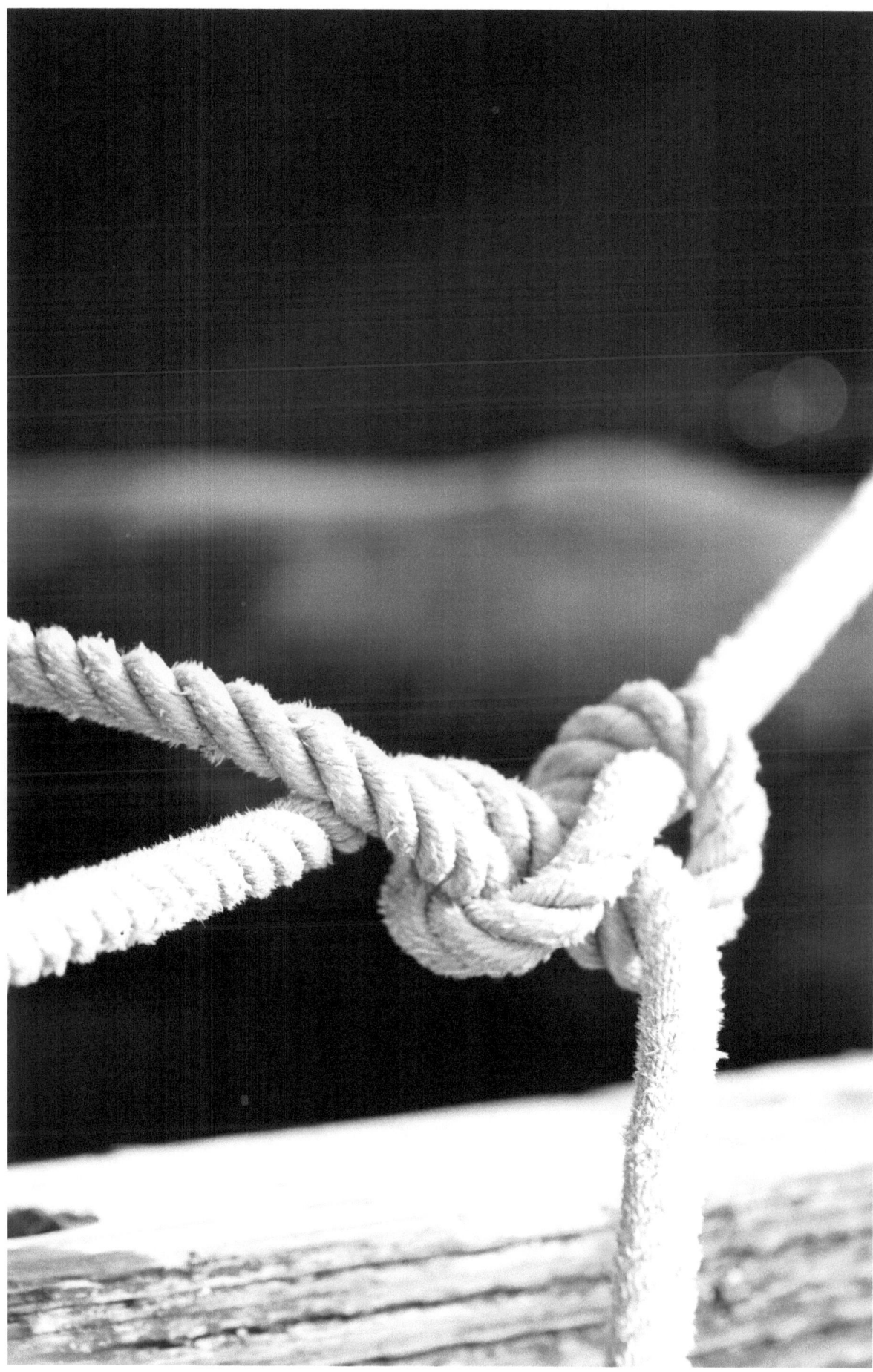

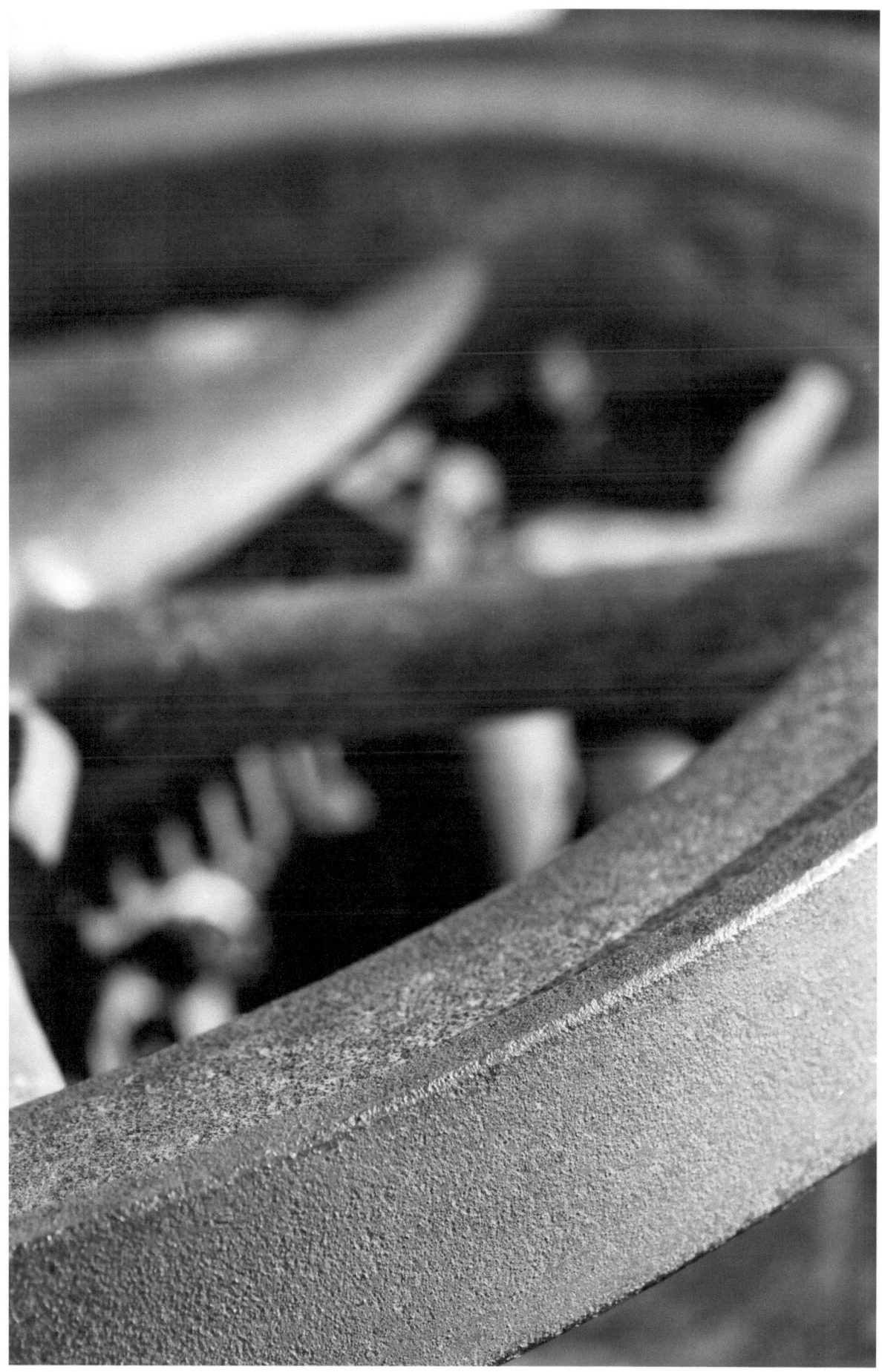

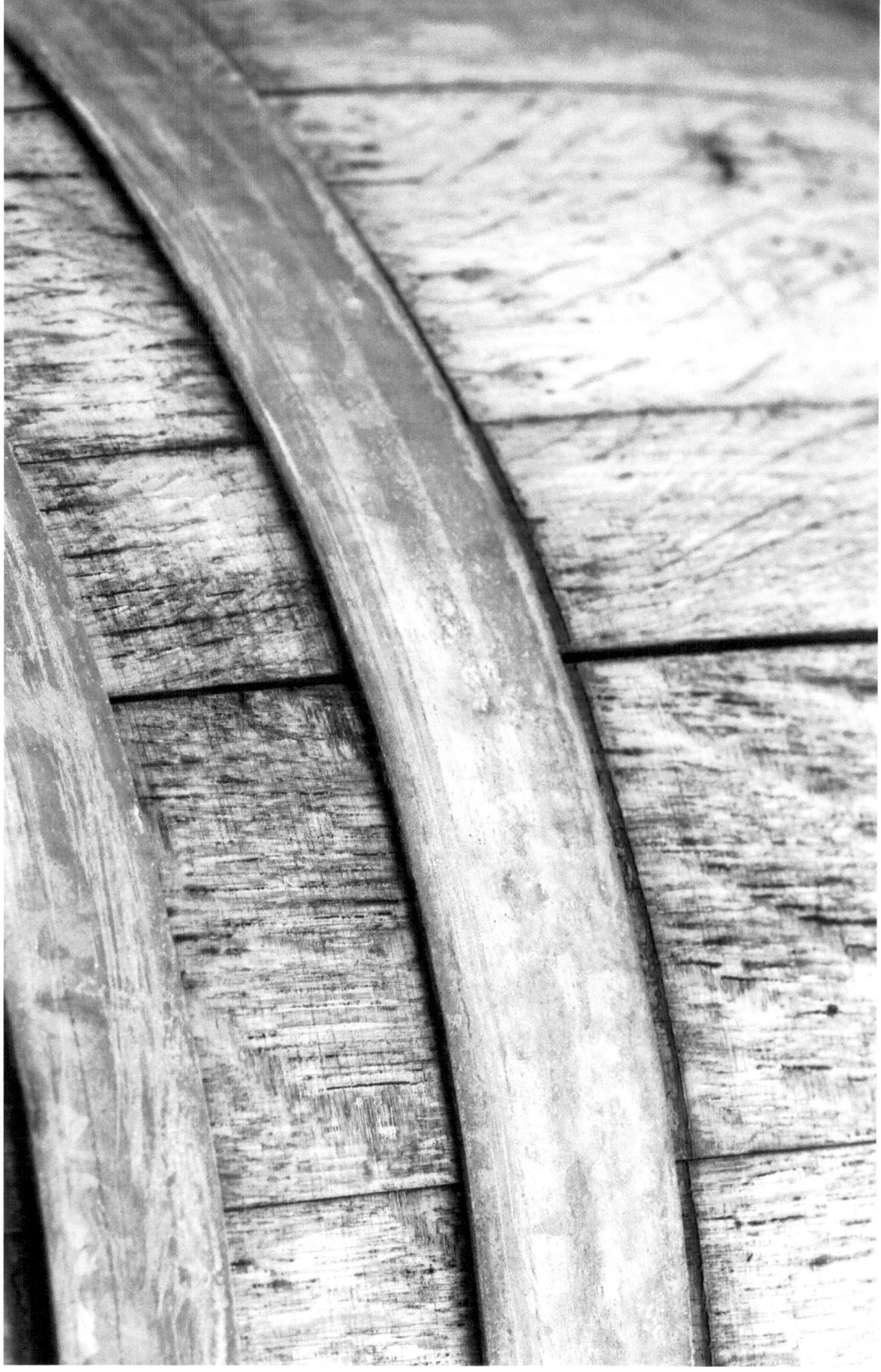

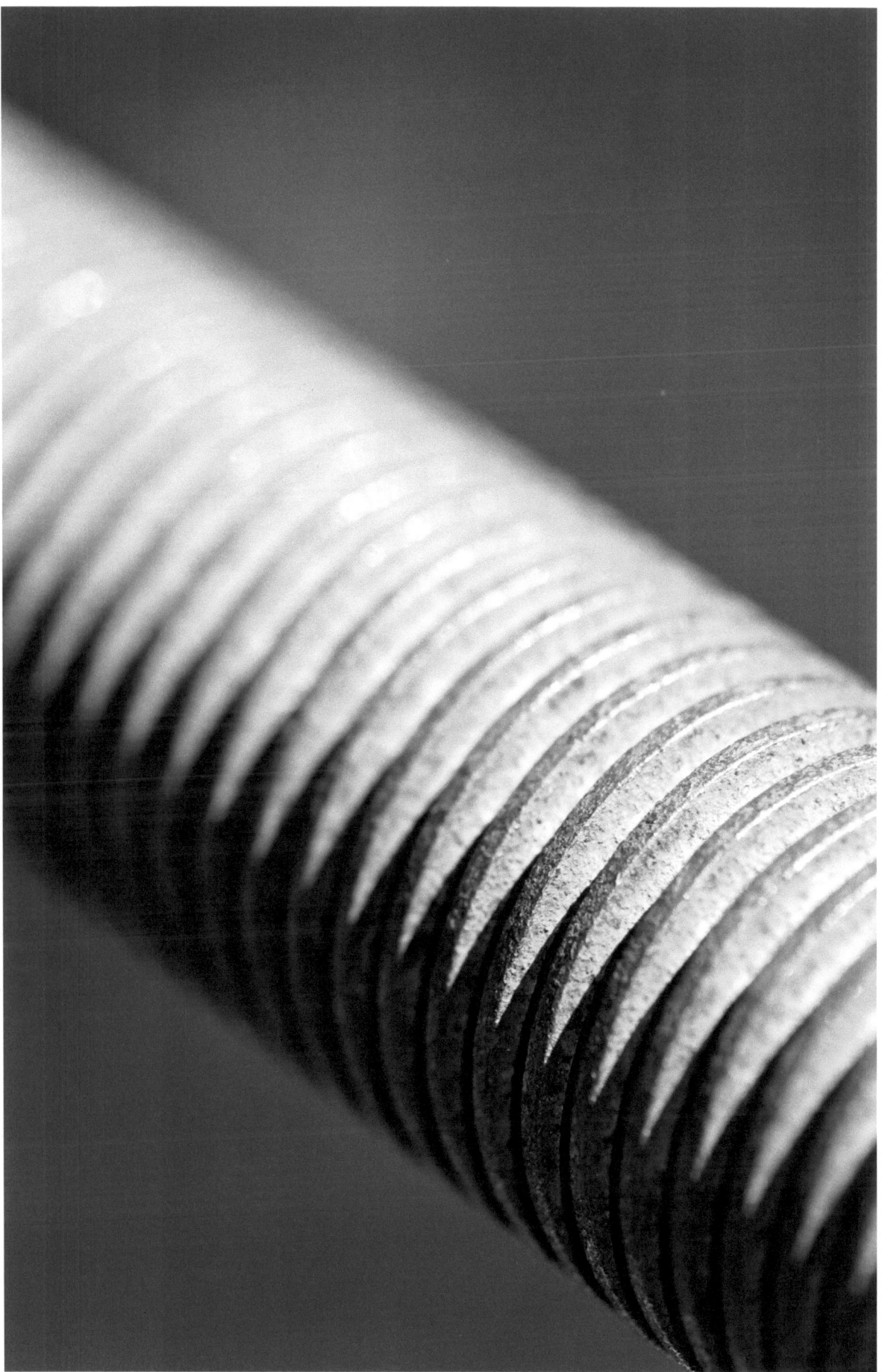

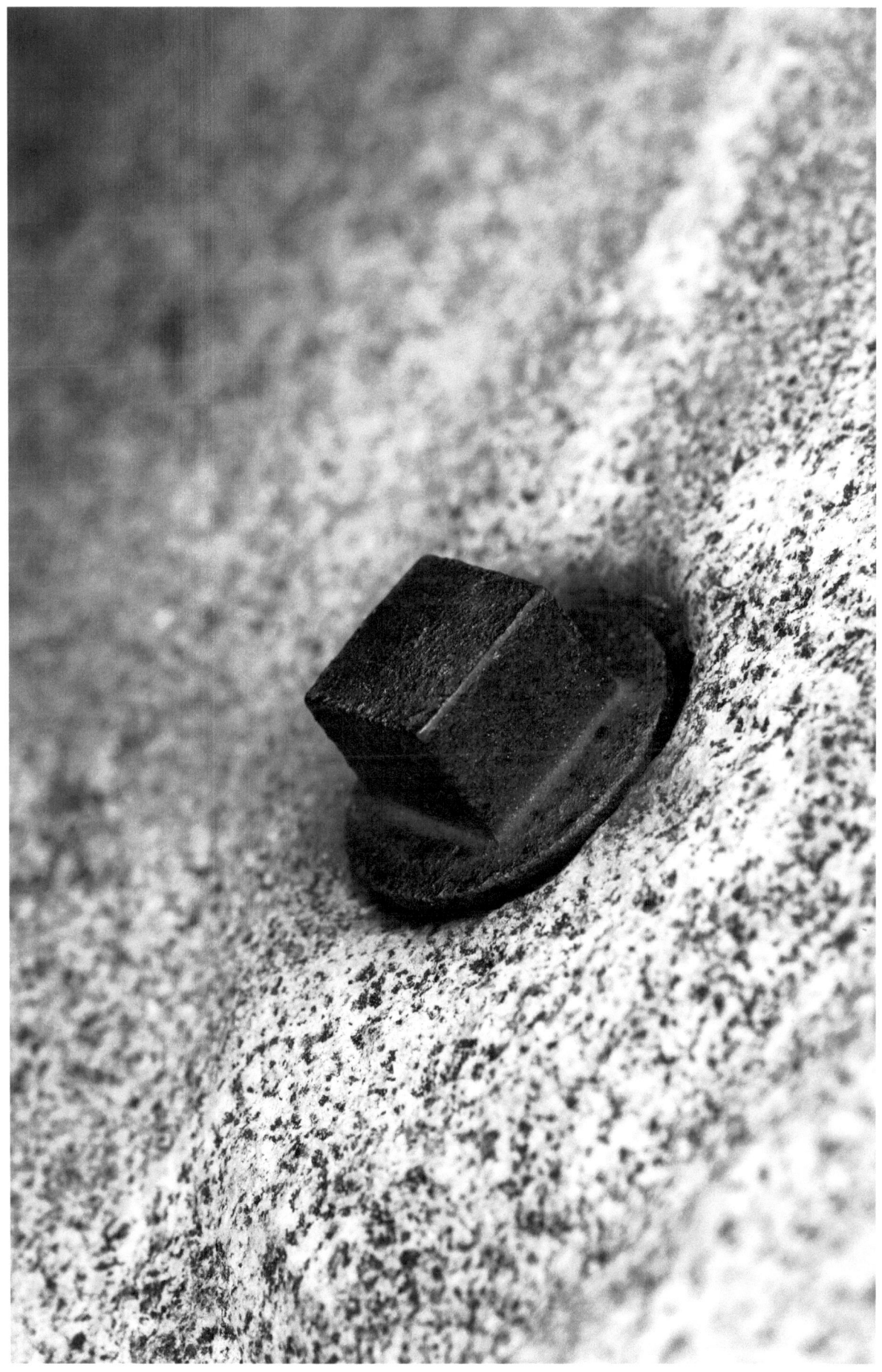

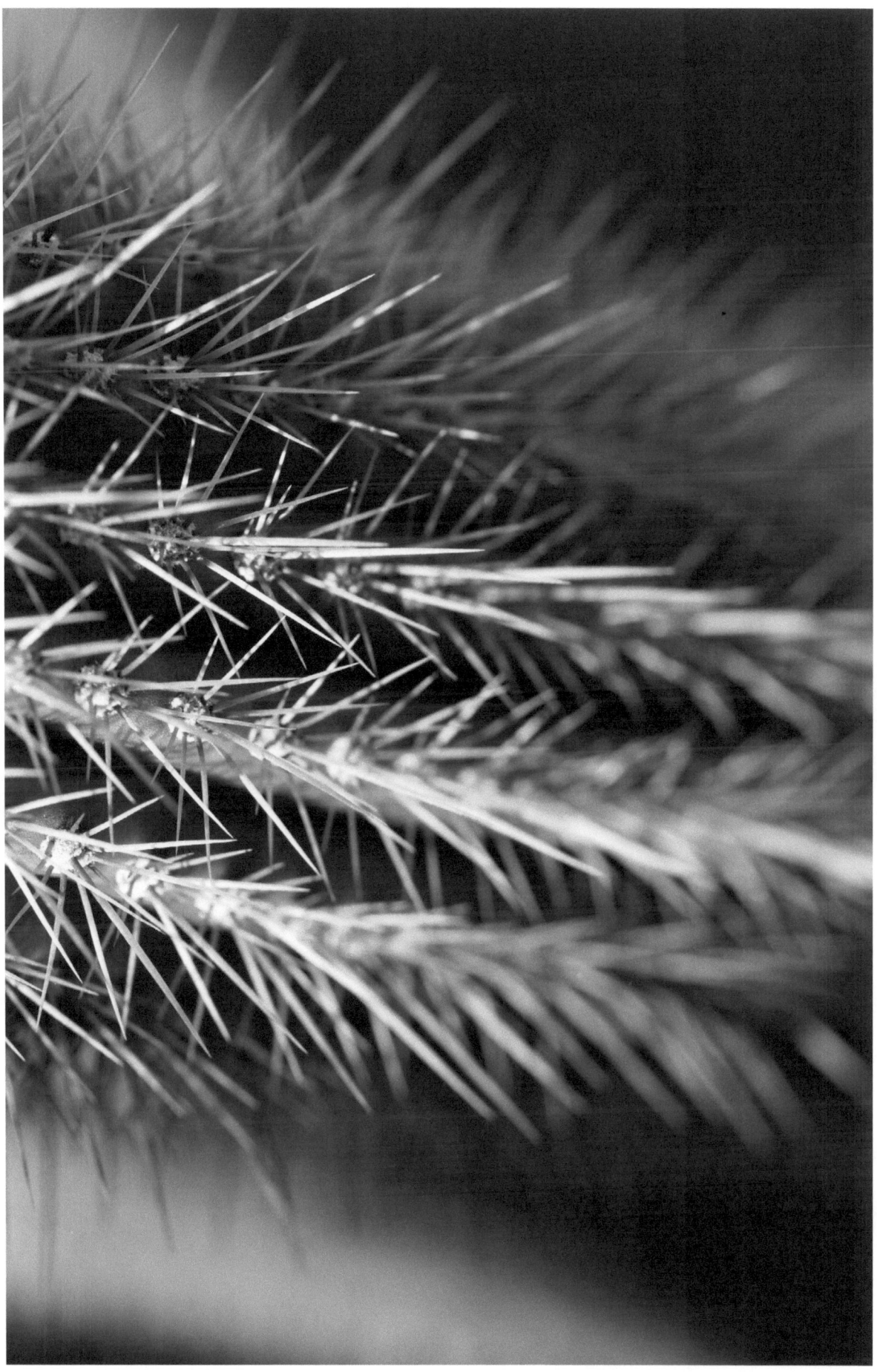

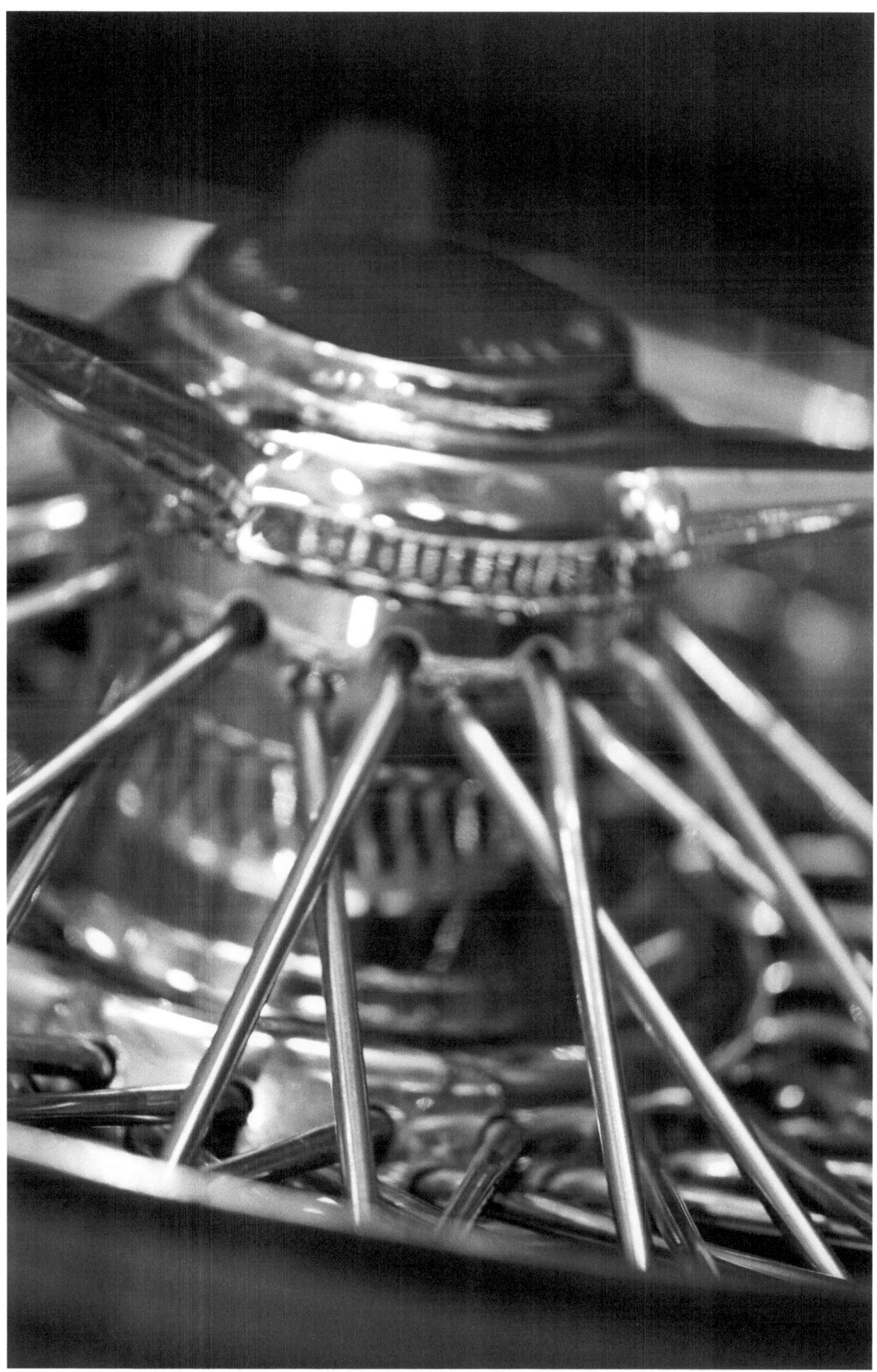

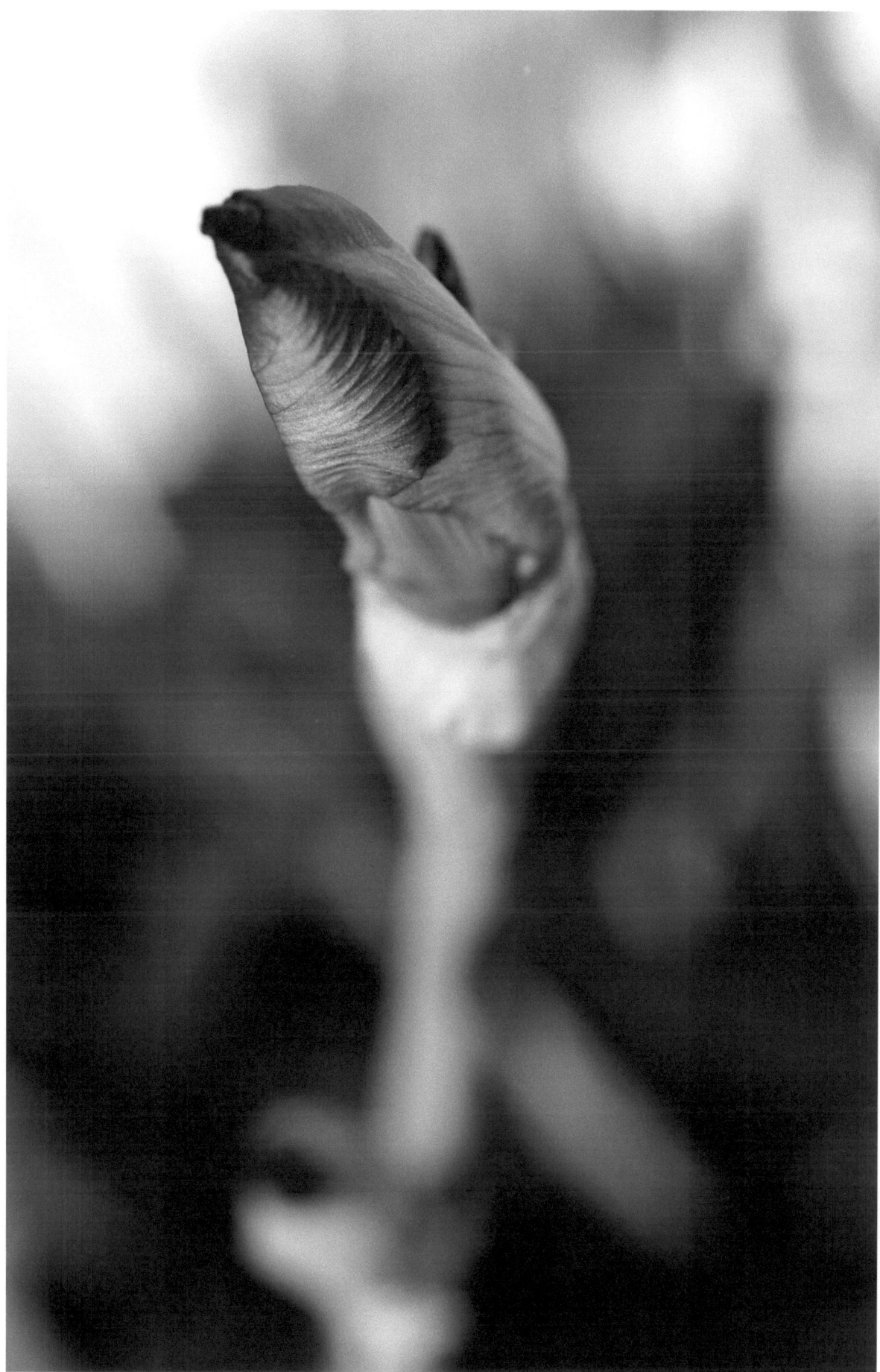

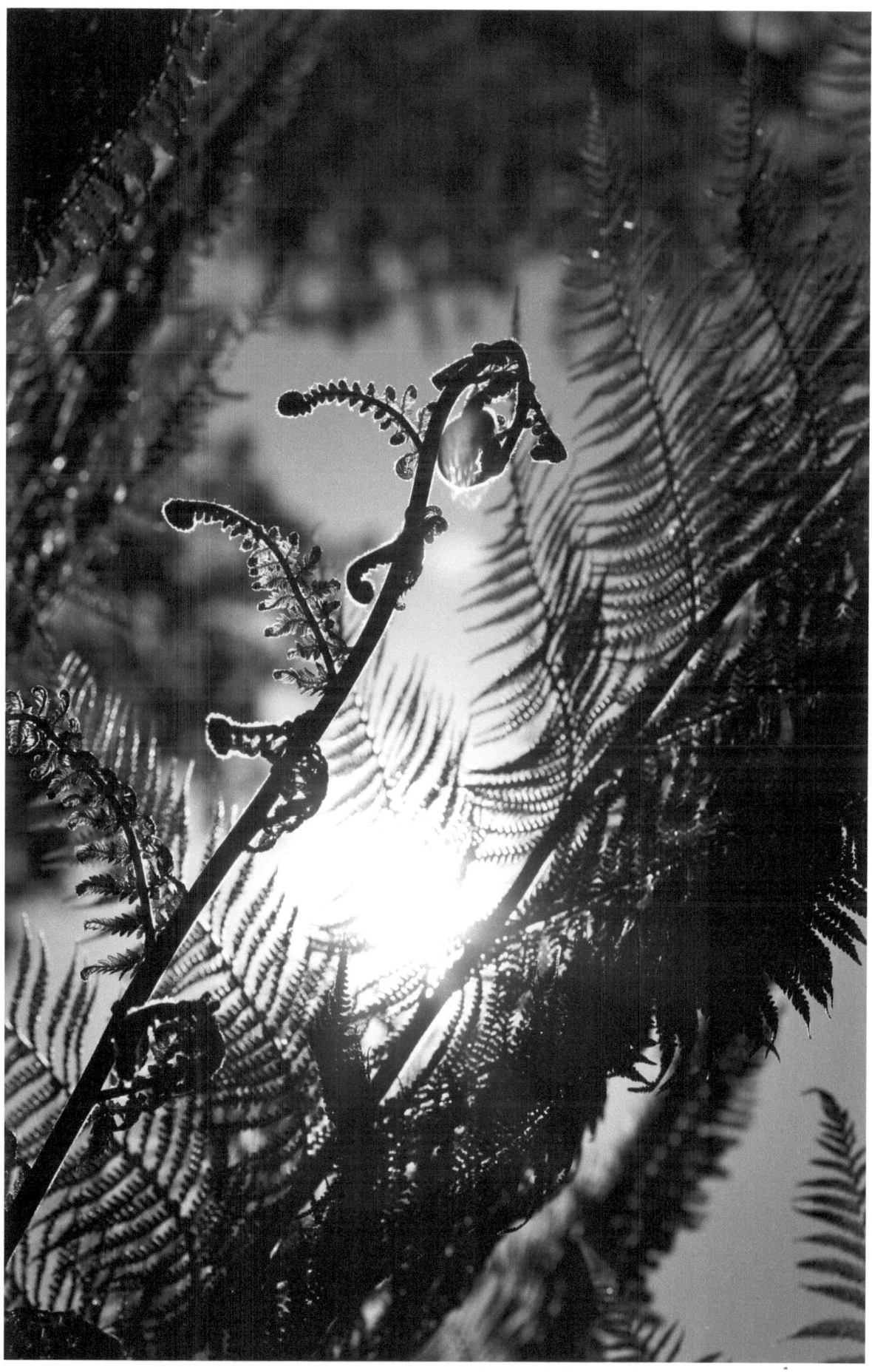

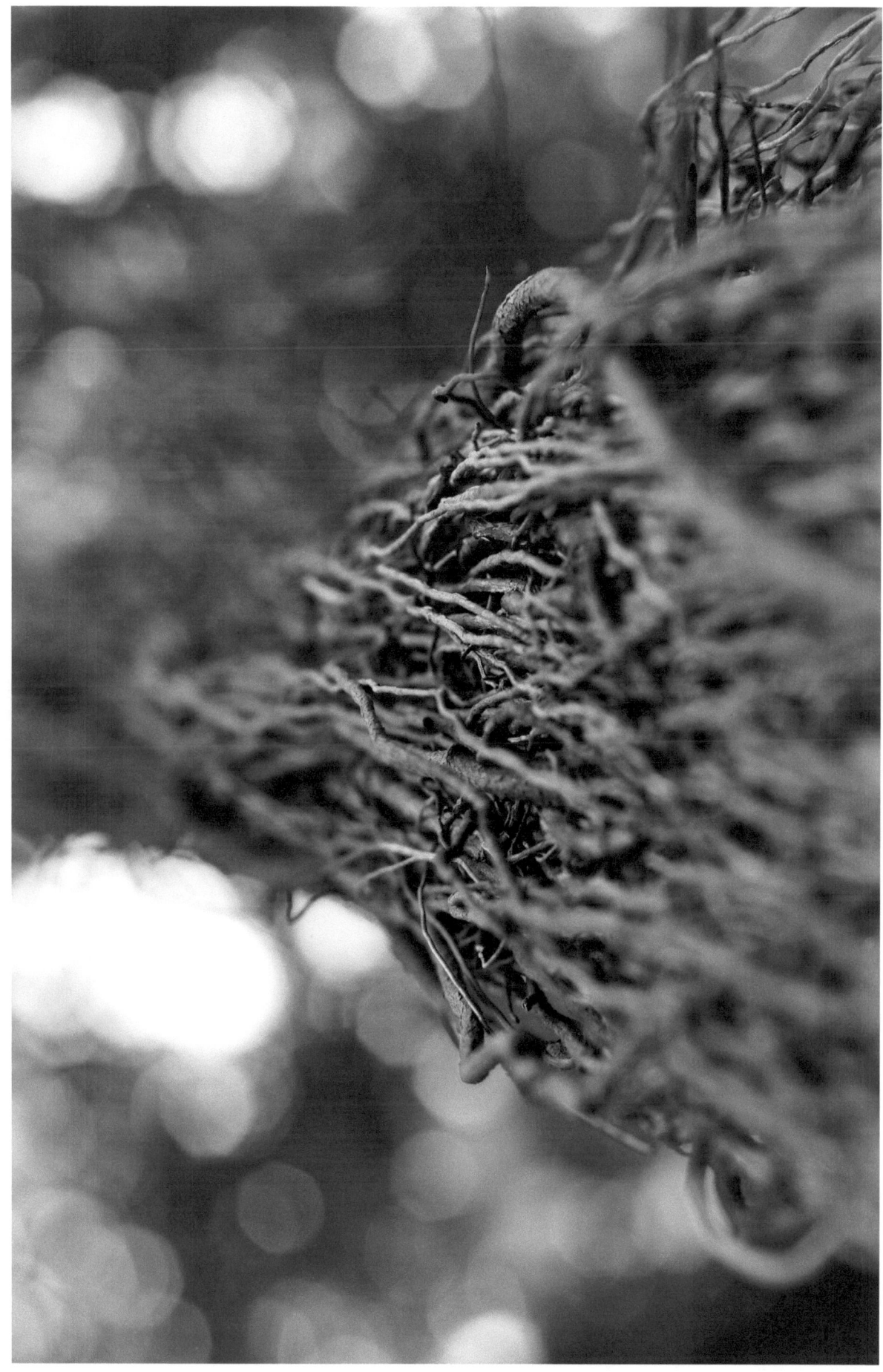

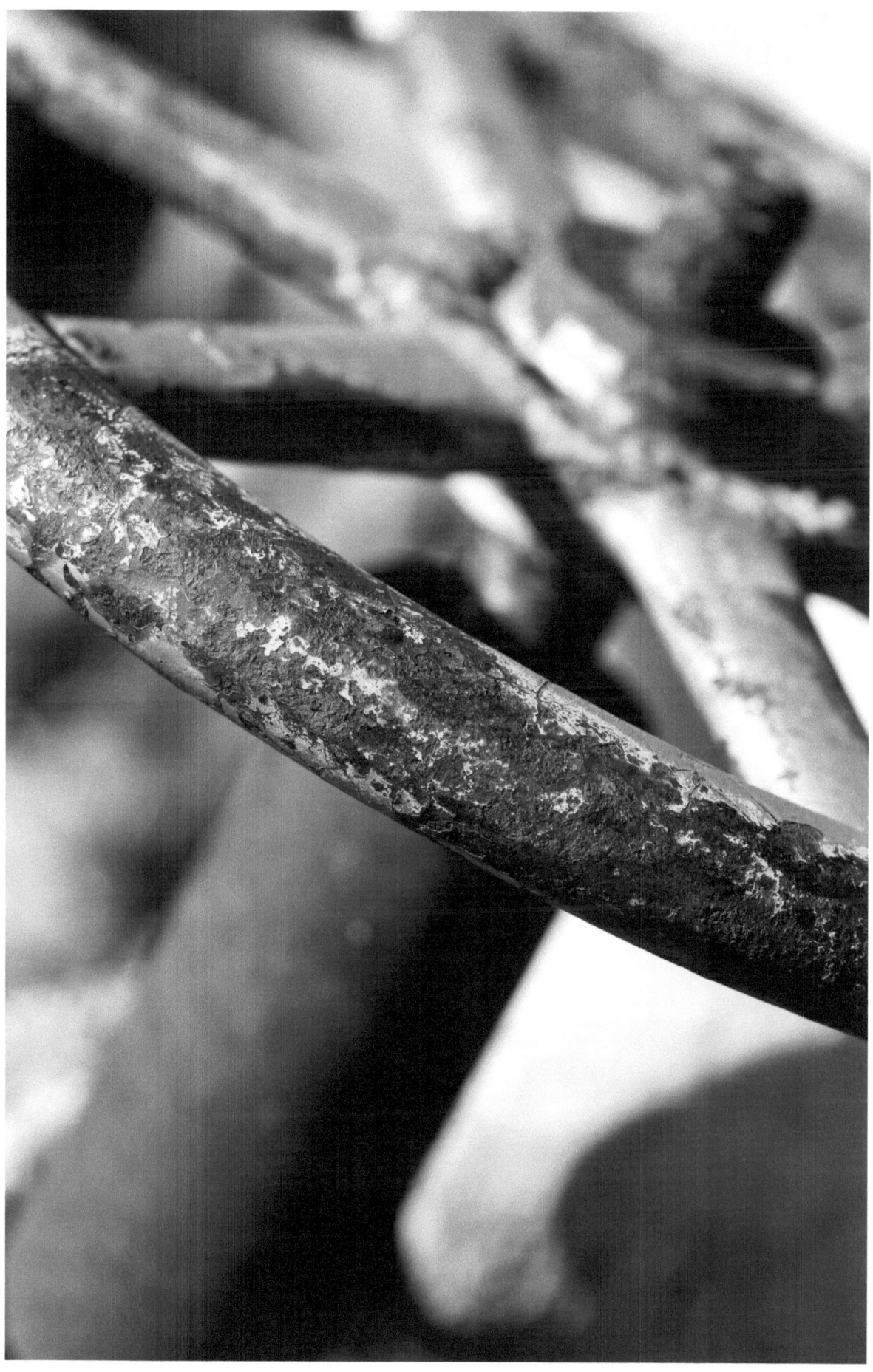

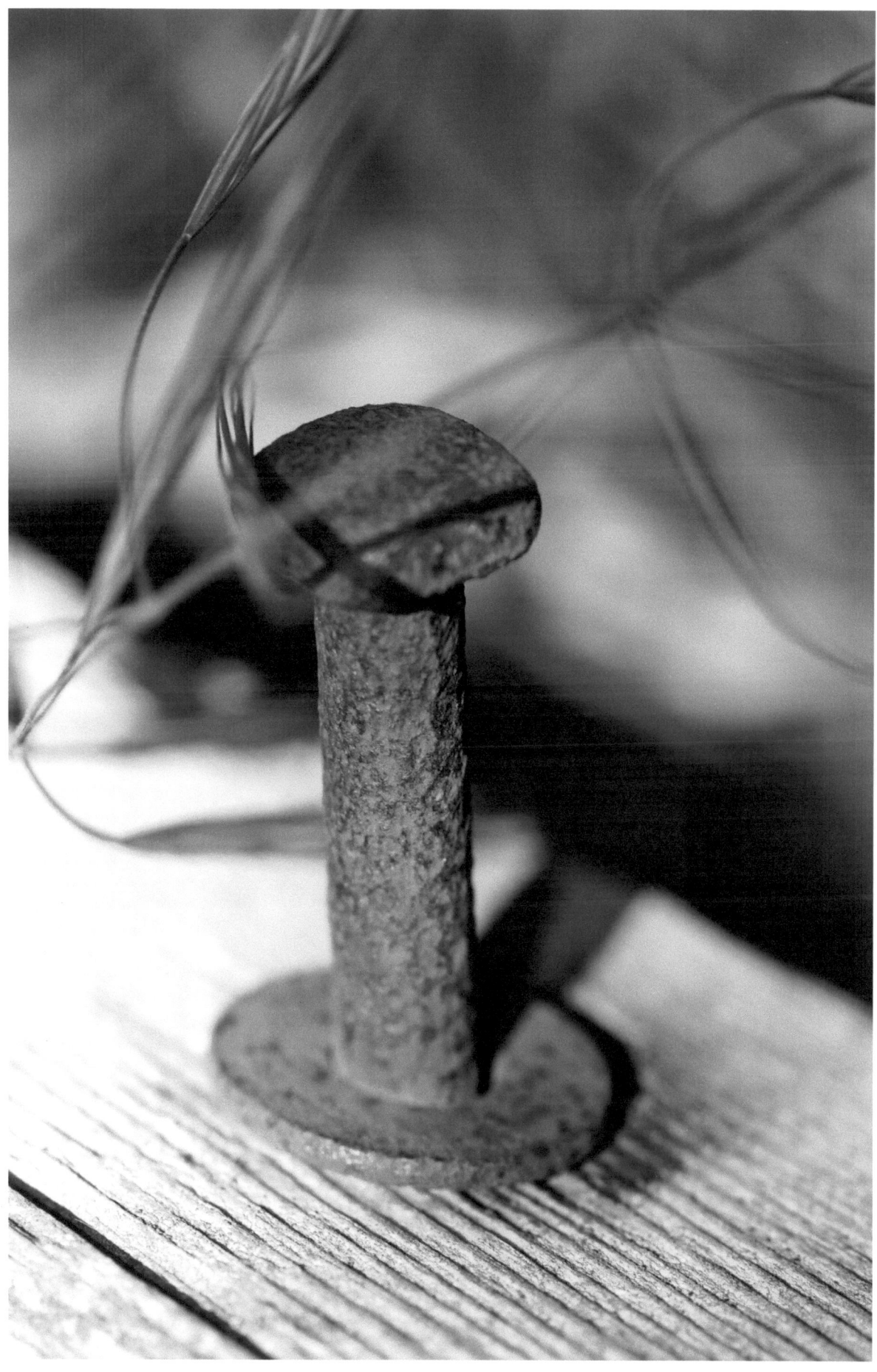

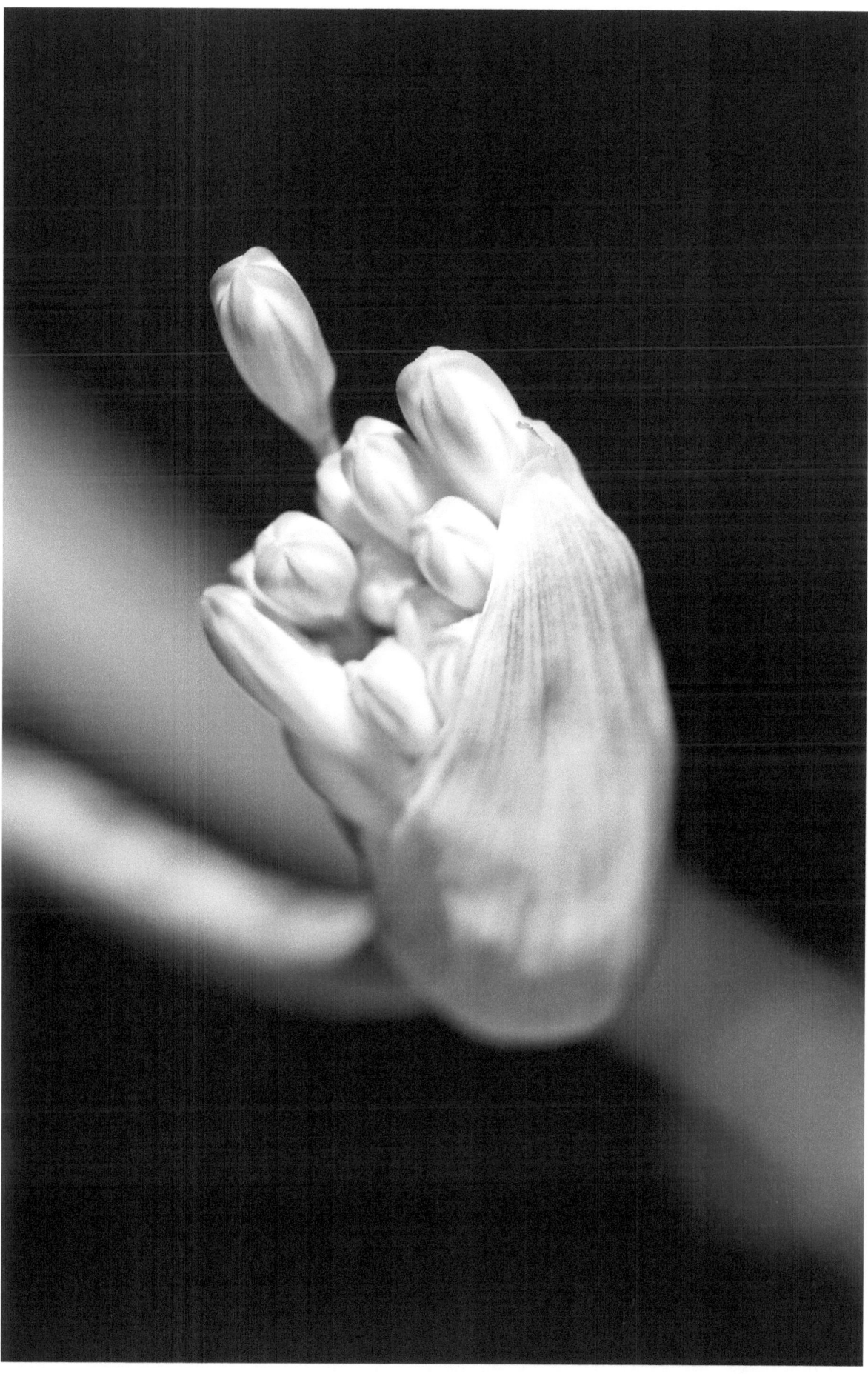

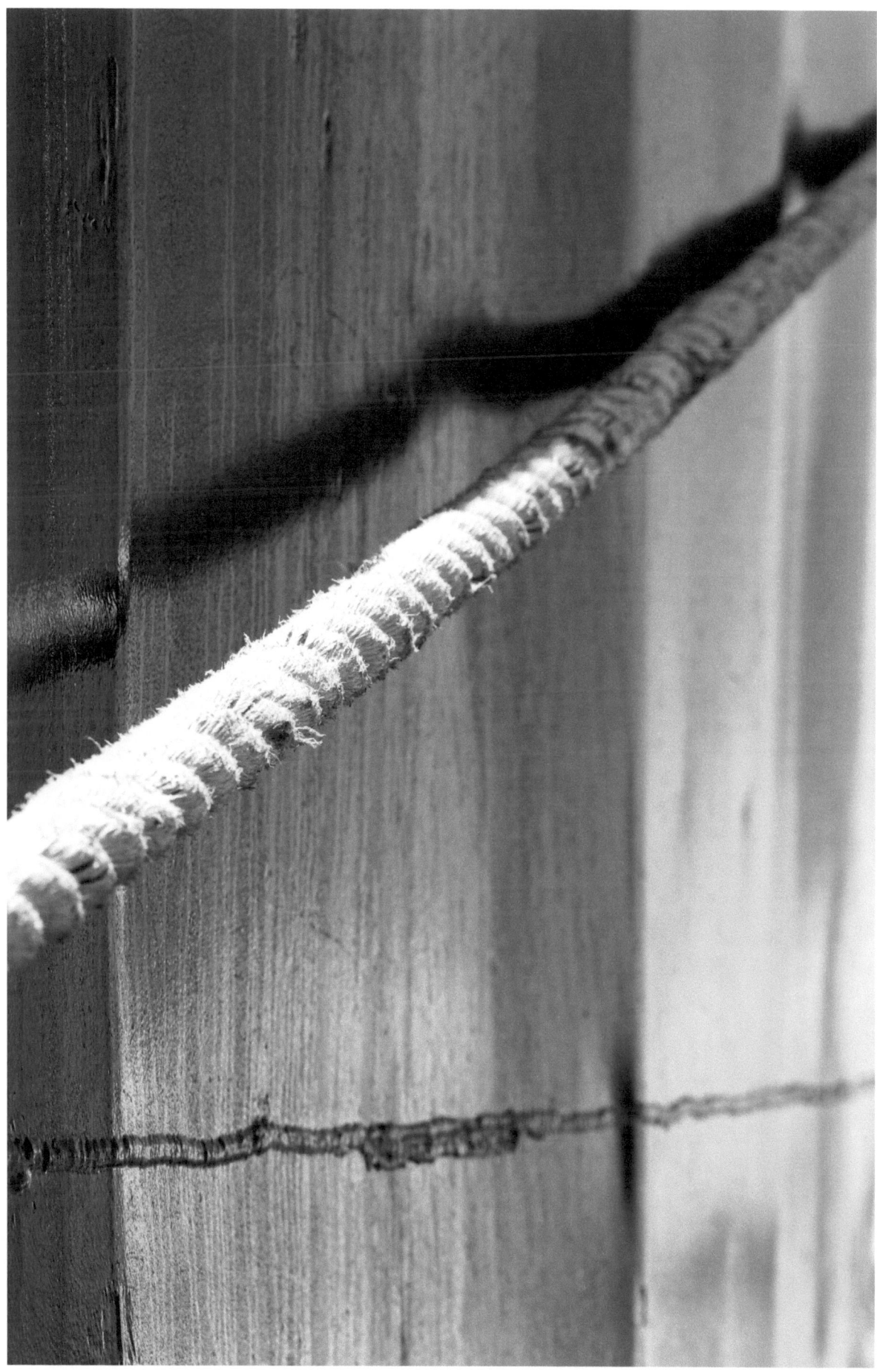

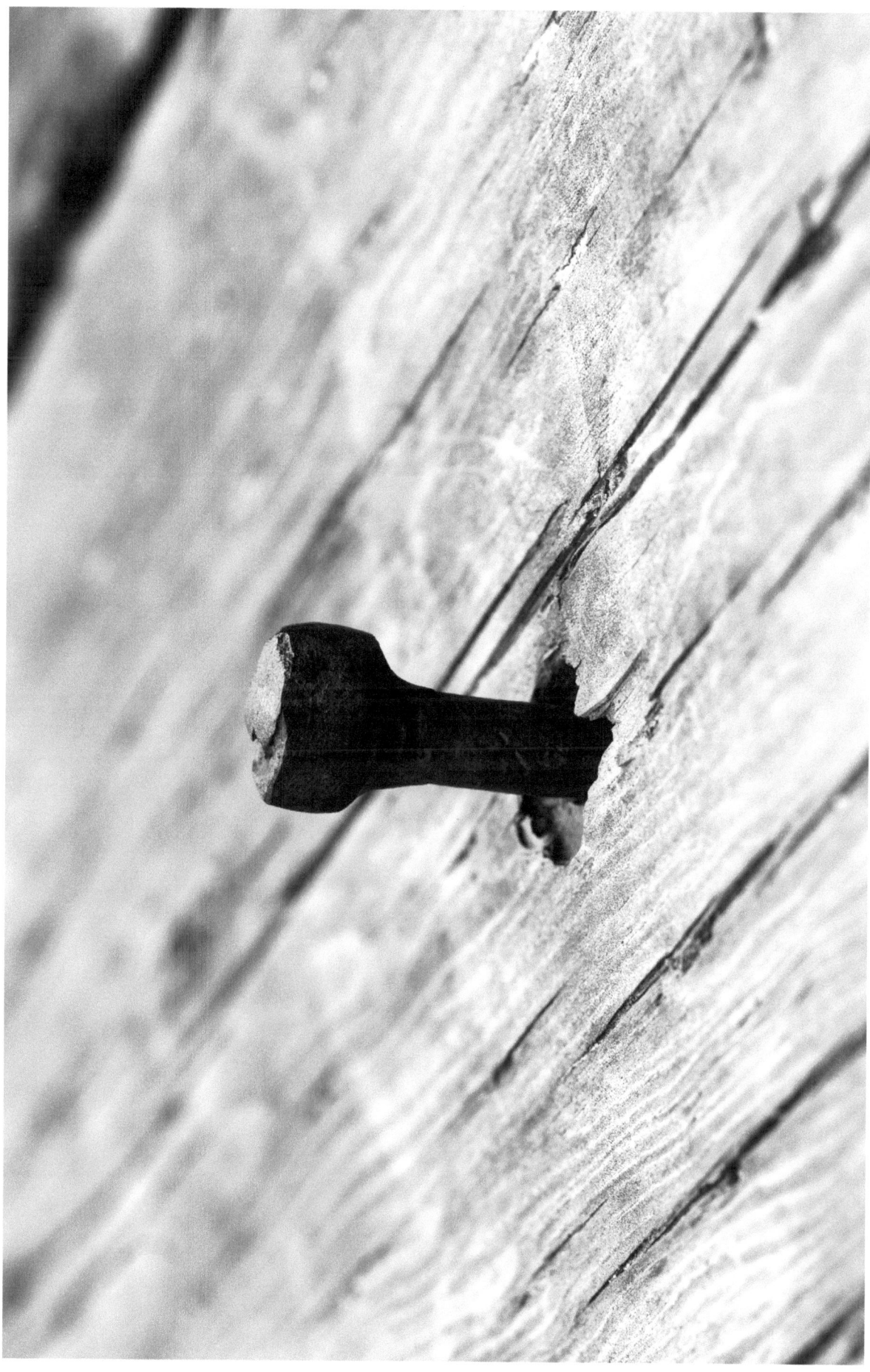

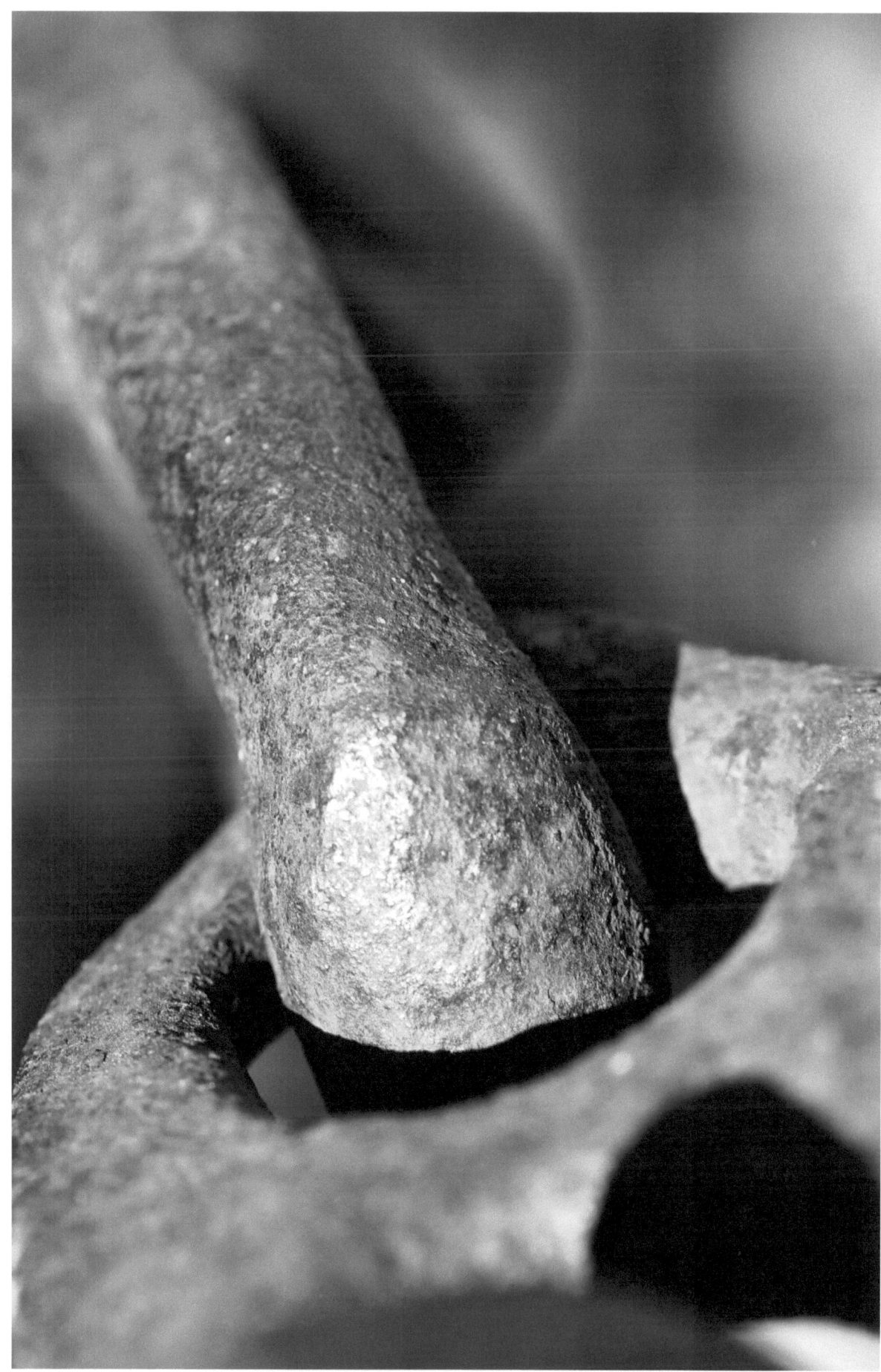

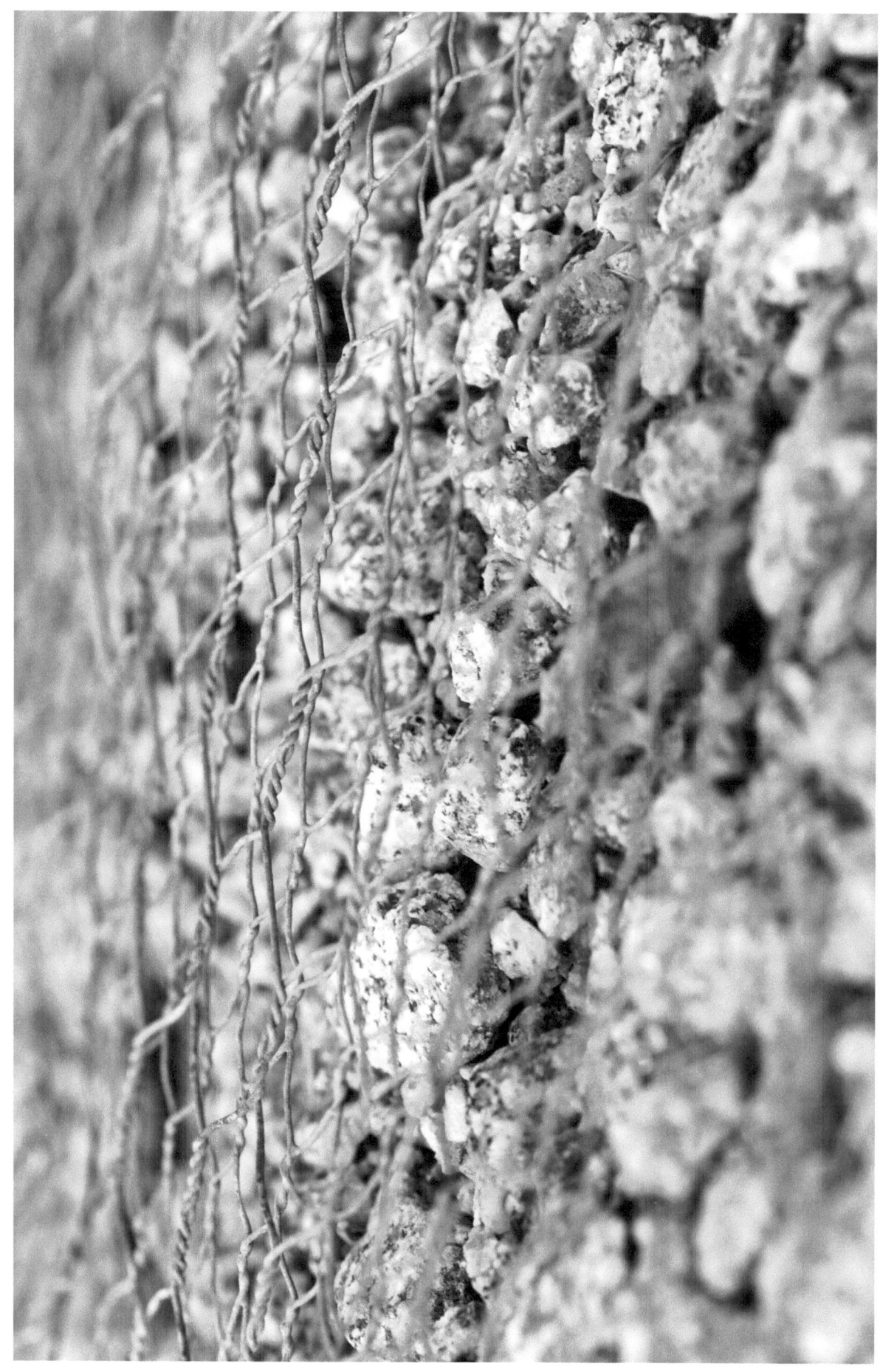

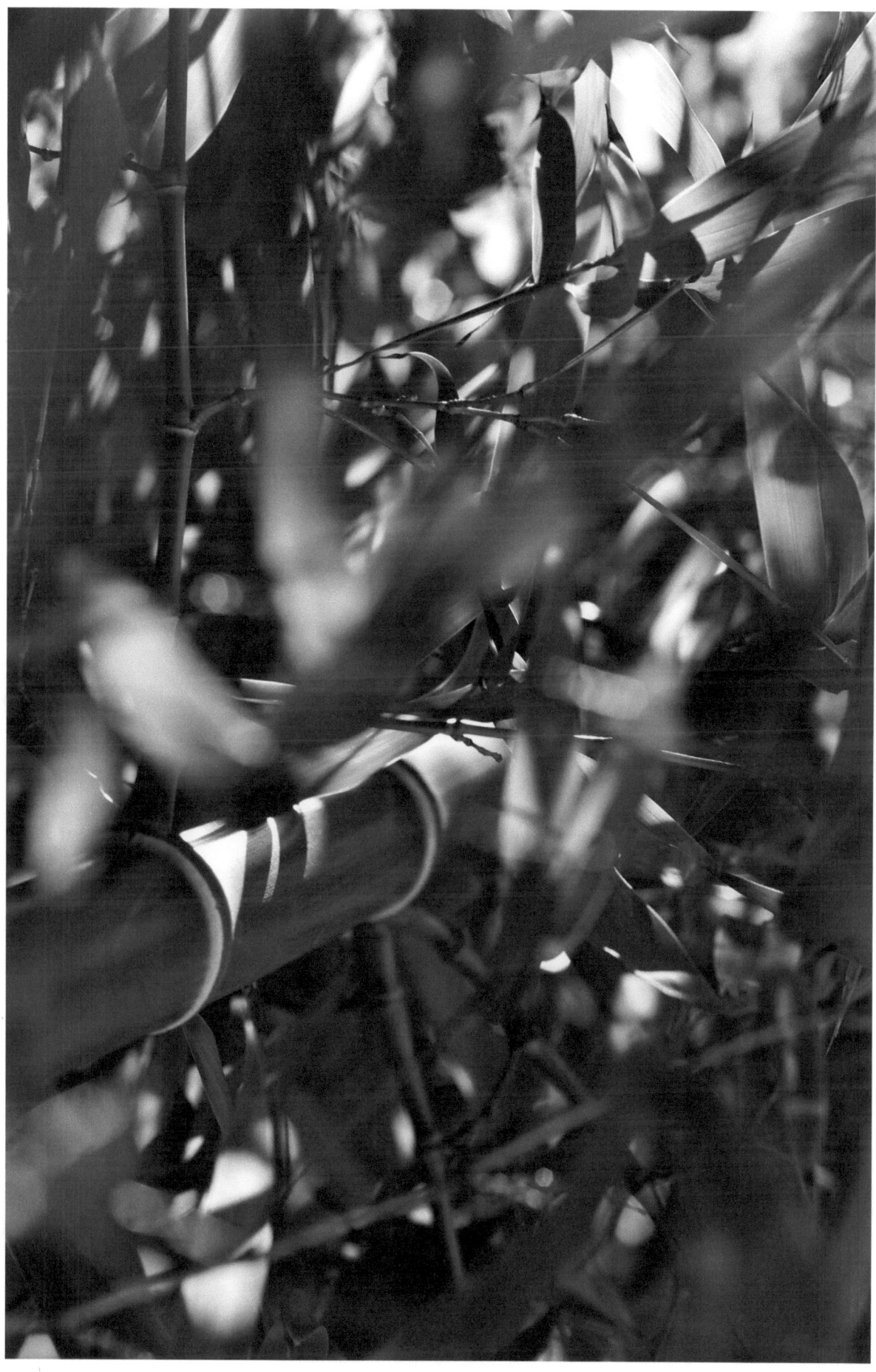

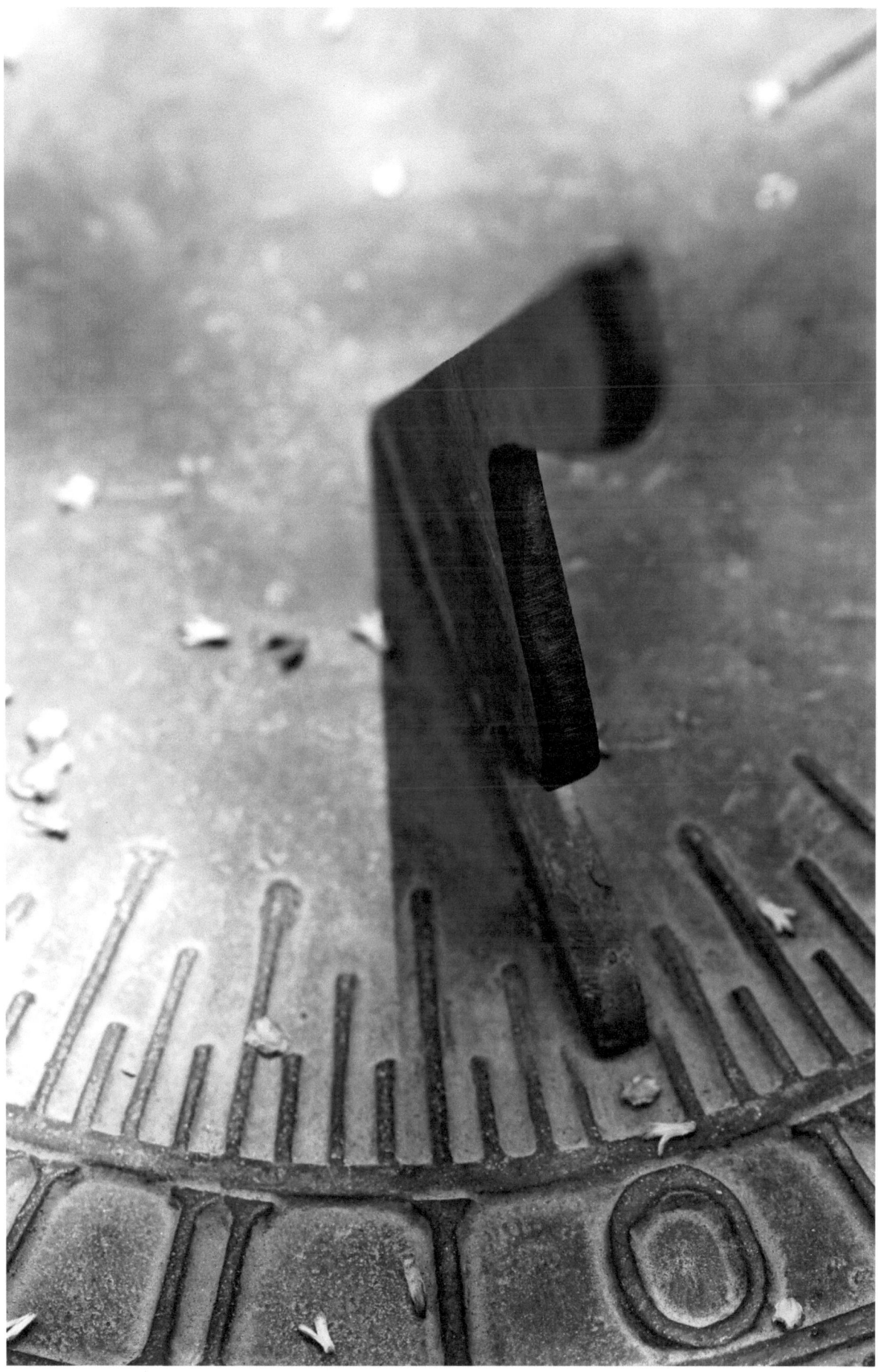

www.ingramcontent.com/pod-product-compliance
Lightning Source LLC
Chambersburg PA
CBHW050815180526
45159CB00004B/1681